Trans4med 4life

Transformation is from the inside out, what you think is what you do.

by Caryl
Pendragon Publishing Group, LLC
© 2018

## ACKNOWLEDGEMENTS

I would like to thank God for His Word that inspired me, His strength that enabled me and His love that encouraged me to write this.

I would also like to thank my family and friends that encouraged me to go forward and celebrated with me as I completed this work.

This is dedicated to you.
Wishing you much success on your journey to true transformation!

# Contents

| | |
|---|---|
| ACKNOWLEDGEMENTS | 2 |
| INTRODUCTION | 5 |
| IS IT FOR APPEARANCES ONLY? | 7 |
| CHANGE VS. TRANSFORMATION | 10 |
| KILLING THE MYTHS | 14 |
| AND ABOLISHING THE STEREOTYPES | 14 |
| MANTRA VS MOTTO | 25 |
| BREAKING THE SILENCE | 29 |
| YOUR TRUTH | 37 |
| GOD'S TRUTH OF YOU | 54 |
| RENEWING THE MIND | 60 |
| GETTING OVER YOURSELF | 63 |
| YOUR TESTIMONY | 69 |
| YOUR COMMUNITY – | 72 |
| WE'RE IN THIS TOGETHER | 72 |
| CONCLUSION | 75 |

# INTRODUCTION

Hi friend,

I've written this book for the person who has made numerous attempts to start, re-start or continue reaching various goals in life and have failed, as I have. Your goal could have been any of the few listed here: financial freedom, owning a business, becoming healthy and/or fit, etc. The list can go on. But this is specifically focused on becoming healthy and/or fit.

You may ask, 'What makes this book different from the millions of others that are available? Are you an expert? Have you ever been certified in the fitness or health industry?'

My approach is a little different, even though there has recently been an influx of material touting transformation in the field. Some have even caught on that transformation is not only a physical change but a mindset change. I don't claim to be an expert in anything, but I have been through the same struggles several times myself and can only give you what I know to be true. I have been a certified personal trainer.

So, here's my hat in the ring to help you to understand not only the difference between change and transformation but to give you a process or principle that will actually help you succeed. The principle of transforming from the inside out is one that can be applied to every area of life. Anything that you may struggle with now can be overcome with true transformation.

## IS IT FOR APPEARANCES ONLY?

*True transformation begins from the inside out. What you think determines what you do. - Caryl*

When most people think about transformation or being transformed, they more than likely think about the physical appearance. Why? We are bombarded with various forms of promotions or marketing tactics for tips, tricks, formulas, programs, and systems that offer some transformations. They all have the same disclaimer, 'individual results may vary'. This is a true statement because everything's not for everybody. Some people do get the expected results. And there are those who don't. It doesn't matter if they've followed the programs, taken the pills, eaten the right number of calories, etc. They still didn't get the expected results. Why? Have you or anyone you know ever enrolled in a fitness program and quit? Have you or anyone you know ever purchased a gym membership and only used it once or a dozen times? Have you or anyone you know purchased the latest and greatest pill/powder that promised transformation within a certain period of time and after the time was up, there were still no significant results? Again, everything's not for everybody. What works for one person may not work for another.

The journey to better health and wellness is individual. You may go on a diet with a friend, or take a class at the gym with a group. But the results you get from either are from your own personal, individual efforts. Having a friend or group is a great way to find support, because they hold you accountable for your progress. I've found that if a person is held accountable for what they do, it makes them perform at a much higher level.

As I journeyed towards better health and wellness, I've tried the new 'it' diet, pill, system, and fitness program. I've experienced more results with some products/systems than others. And with some, I've experienced no results. I gave up in some instances and in others, I pushed my way through to the finish. But the reality of it all is that I was still no closer to where I wanted to be than when I started my journey (over, and over, and over) again. Each effort to change for the better was begun with the right mindset, motivation, and approach. However, once I saw change, I could never maintain it. The changes I experienced were temporary.

I'm not saying that any of the various methods I tried didn't work.  What I'm saying is there was something within me that wouldn't allow for any change to be permanent.  Can you say frustrating?

I'm not the only person who's experienced this frustration.  If I were, there would be no successful health/wellness businesses.  Everyone would be healthy and fit, except for me.  We know that isn't true.  That's why I needed to tell you that you've not suffered anything that someone else hasn't experienced.  Trust me, you're not alone.

## CHANGE VS. TRANSFORMATION

The below answer to the question of 'What's the difference between change and transformation?' clearly states my thoughts almost exactly. So much so, that I had to share it with you.

*[Sriidhar Ramakrishnan](), Co-founder & CEO at Maptech Infosoft (1998-present)*

*Change is what happens to us by force or by circumstances or with desperate effort by one person or a group of people. Transformation, on the other hand, is by passion or with a willing attitude or willful act with self-interest, to work on ourselves to become what we have to become progressively. Change may not last forever as it keeps evolving or devolving, whereas transformation is a dimensional shift, and once we are transformed there is no question of going back but being a transformed person. Change is only temporary. Whereas "Permanent Change is Transformation". @36 Golden Rules by M.K Anand, [anand@seechangeworld.com](mailto:anand@seechangeworld.com)*

Have you ever looked in the mirror and said, 'I really need to get back into shape.'? 'Look at how big you are.' Have you told people, 'I don't take pictures because I look like a cow.'? Have you ever told friends or coworkers that you're on a diet and eat salads, etc. while in their presence and go home or on the way home, binge on everything that you've stayed away from all day?

I'm very familiar with these scenarios because I've said and done them all. Why am I sharing this? Well, I'm not the only person who has suffered from bad body image or low self-esteem. What does either have to do with transformation? Give me a few more minutes of your time and you'll see.

Here we are looking for that perfect plan or system that will help us transform our bodies into the image we've had in our heads for a long time. Some people are trying to find the program or system that will help them let the skinny person out. Oops! Did I say that? Yup, sure did.

What makes you think a skinny person is living inside you? It's not the skinny person that needs to be let out. It's your mind that needs to be freed so you can accept and love yourself. The focus should be on becoming healthy and well as opposed to becoming skinny.

*'Everybody's not meant to be a size 0 or 3. Being healthy at any size is what matters.' – Caryl* Many people are looking for a quick change and aren't willing to put in the work it takes to transform. Yes, transformation takes time. You must trust the process.

If you just want change, continue to seek programs and systems that can get that for you over the course of a few months. Just a reminder, the changes you get are not permanent. If you're not careful, you'll spend a lot of money trying to maintain your results.

Another truth in the industry is, if you do something for 21 days, it becomes a habit. For example, if you replace the chips you snack on with a piece of fruit instead, you'll most likely not choose chips as a snack and go for the fruit. Again, it works for some people and not others.

You can change the way you think and still end up back on square one. What we think changes with any situation or circumstance. Not saying that people are indecisive, but for doing better and getting better, very few people get on that road. Why? That road is hard and lonely. Yes, I said lonely. Whatever you do to better your life is all up to your efforts, not the efforts of someone else. It's your energy, the fight in you that will determine your success. God will place people in your life to help you along the way, but the ultimate deciding factor lies within you.

## KILLING THE MYTHS
## AND ABOLISHING THE STEREOTYPES

In this section, we will address a few myths and stereotypes that surround the health and fitness industry.

What is a myth? According to Merriam Webster, a myth is a popular belief or tradition that has grown up around something or someone. (Thin/skinny people are healthy.)

What is a stereotype? Again, according to Merriam Webster, a stereotype is something conforming to a fixed or general pattern; *a standardized mental picture that is held in common by members of a group and the represents an oversimplified opinion, prejudiced attitude, or uncritical judgment.* (Fitness trainers and health coaches must be slim to be good or effective.)

What's the first thing that comes to mind when you hear the word diet? Eating rabbit food, drinking like ten gallons of water a day and a lot of 'can't haves'. Who wants that?

What's the first thing that comes to mind when you hear the word exercise? Hours at the gym, ultra-muscular trainers that scream at you to 'Do one more!' Or, what about the super slim trainer that has energy for days while you're on your last leg after the first five minutes? Let's not forget the after-work out pain and soreness. I'm not saying you won't run into trainers exactly as I described, but that's not how most trainers are. But the ones who are like that have given trainers a bad reputation! Lol.

These stereotypes make one reconsider their choice to either diet or exercise. These are the hurdles we must overcome to motivate ourselves to start or restart our journey to better health and fitness.

What do myths and stereotypes have to do with being transformed for life? Again, it's what we think about a thing that determines how much we involve ourselves or not. Some myths and stereotypes can negatively affect our perception of diets and exercise, while some may offer a positive outcome and yet still be wrong. I intend to give you the truth.

Let's look at an excerpt from the WebMD article "Top 9 Fitness Myths – Busted" written by Colette Bouchez who interviewed professional athlete and personal coach Eric Harr, author of *The Portable Personal Trainer*; Todd Schlifstein, DO, a clinical instructor at New York University Medical Center's Rusk Institute (at the time of this article. He is now affiliated with Lenox Hill Hospital and NYU Langone Medical Center) and Phil Tyne, director of the fitness center at the Baylor Tom Landry Health & Wellness Center in Dallas.

1. *Swimming is a great weight loss activity, right?*

    While swimming is great for increasing lung capacity, toning muscles, and even helping to burn off excess tension, Harr says the surprising truth is that unless you are swimming for hours a day, it may not help you lose much weight.

    "Because the buoyancy of the water is supporting your body, you're not working as hard as it would if, say, you were moving on your own steam -- like you do when you run," says Harr.

    Further, he says, it's not uncommon to feel ravenous when you come out of the water.

"It may actually cause you to eat more than you normally would, so it can make it harder to stay with an eating plan," he says.

2. *If you're not working up a sweat, you're not working hard enough.*
"[Sweating](#) is not necessarily an indicator of exertion," says Tyne. "[Sweating](#) is your body's way of cooling itself."

It's possible to burn a significant number of calories without breaking a sweat: Try taking a walk or doing some light [weight training](#).

3. *Doing crunches or working on an 'ab machine' will get rid of belly fat.*
Don't believe everything you hear on those late-night infomercials! Harr says that while an ab-crunching device might "help strengthen the muscles around your midsection and improve your posture," being able to "see" your abdominal muscles has to do with your overall percentage of body fat. If you don't lose the belly fat, he says, you won't see the ab muscles.

> But can doing ab crunches help you to lose that belly fat? Experts say no.
>
> "You can't pick and choose areas where you'd like to burn fat," says Phil Tyne, director of the fitness center at the Baylor Tom Landry Health & Wellness Center in Dallas. So, crunches aren't going to target weight loss in that area.
>
> "In order to burn fat, you should create a workout that includes both cardiovascular and strength-training elements. This will decrease your overall body fat content," including the area around your midsection, he says.

I can say I have met amazing trainers and I've met some that weren't so amazing, but they were trainers just the same. Each trainer has his or her own style and no two are the same. There are plenty of fitness trainers and health coaches who aren't super slim or abundantly muscular. They look just like you and me. Never judge a book by its cover, it may surprise you. You never know if the person standing in front of you has a health issue that requires them to be on medication that adds on weight, but they still show up energized and ready to help you get the results you're looking for.

So, as you look for a fitness trainer or fitness coach, look for one that offers programs that will suit your particular style and will get you the best results possible, safely! This means that the person you sign up with will encourage you to challenge yourself, tell you the truth about the best diet for you, and will guide through a balance of body/goal specific exercises that will help you reach your personal health and fitness goals.

Remember that no one is perfect and as you search for a trainer/coach, you may run across someone who's a beginner in the business and yet they know everything they need to know to help you. Allow a newbie to put all those hours of study to practice (with a discount) as they lead you to better health and fitness. (Had to put a plug in for the newbies.)

So, how do we get past the stereotypes? We get past the stereotypes by turning the microscope on ourselves. Are we seeing trainers the way we want to be seen – as individuals and not as a one-size fits all category? If you attend a group exercise class, you know that everyone in the class differs from yourself. So, why would you try to categorize a trainer or coach as a one-size fits all? See that person as an individual, just like you want to be seen as an individual uniquely different from everyone else in the group. Don't do yourself a disservice by overlooking someone's skills based on their looks. Take the time to see what they have to offer for your particular needs by sitting down and explaining what your areas of concern are and what results you expect at the end of your training program.

Ok, so that's been said, I will share my experience with the stereotypical fitness trainer image.

I had just finished my training as an aerobic step instructor and was given a great opportunity to substitute when the regular trainer needed to be off for a group of eight to ten ladies (mostly elderly). I was a size twelve, I was ok but not in great shape. The regular trainer was a super slim size three who couldn't have weighed more than ninety-nine lbs. soaking wet. I mention this because the regular trainer was built like the other six members of the instructor class I had just finished. I was the biggest in the class which was fine by me because I had the mindset that people could relate to me because they would be able to see that we were in it together. But these women were brutal. They would snicker and whisper if I made a misstep or breathed harder than them. They would basically ignore me until I made a mistake. That was a humbling experience for me. I didn't allow them to see that their bad behavior bothered me because I had goals to meet and getting certified was step one. Anyway, so the first day I showed up to observe the class I participated by doing the modified versions of the exercises, the women were looking at me funny. When the regular trainer, let's call her Tracy, advised them I would sub for her, one lady said, 'You look like you belong in the class and not teaching it. You're just as big as the rest of us. How are you going to teach us anything?' Can you feel the heat of embarrassment rising within? Well, I did. Here I was all excited and smiling from ear to ear because I was so pumped to finally do what I've always wanted to do, and she says this just as bluntly and nonchalant. I was floored! Her words were like a slap in the face. I kept the smile, it was a little hard now and harder to hold with everyone watching and waiting for me to respond. I said this to her, "I hope you don't let my size fool you. I am certified and know how to put some pretty basic steps together for a workout. But you all have been doing this a lot longer than me. So, I'm going to need your help when it comes to adding more advanced moves when the routines get old. I also believe that as you see my weight change, you'll be encouraged to continue to come to class and give it your all." That seemed to get their attention, but not their full confidence, yet. I was ok with that, but can I tell you I cried in the bathroom before leaving and again on the way home and then again later that night.

Within a month, I went from being just the sub to teaching the stretch and tone classes two days a week. Before the end of the second month, I was the regular teacher because Tracy had taken a position with a new gym. So, the women were stuck with me even though a few dropped off when Tracy left. That hurt, but I had to grow up and accept that everybody won't like me and just to move on from there.

I taught those lovely ladies for four months before I had to leave and get a job paying real money, unfortunately. I say unfortunately because I was finally self-employed and loving what I did.  I wasn't the best trainer, but I was making progress.

 During the first couple of months, those lovelies complained at first they weren't seeing results. Plus, they were feeling places on their bodies they hadn't felt in a long time. They were used to taking it easy, but I pushed them a little more than they were used to. Whenever I said, "no pain, no gain," they would groan and I would laugh. I had a lot of fun with them. I wanted them to see RESULTS!  Isn't that why they paid their money and came to the classes?  Well, a few ladies complained that I was too hard until they saw RESULTS!

When they complained that the routines were getting old, I held them to what I said to them when we first met.  I had them help coordinate or choreograph the routines.

When they complained about the music, I mixed it up with what they liked and what I liked.

I let them know that I suffered too.  When I told them I felt as much pain as they did, they didn't believe me because I never showed it as I coached them through another workout.  I would sometimes limp into the room and barely be able to move, but once I started the music, all pain disappeared. I would be living for the moment to teach/train. But believe me, once the music stopped, the party was over.

By the time I quit, I was toned and down to a size eight. The ladies that took the class seriously had all dropped two to three sizes and two got rid of some of their daily medications.

But with all that, that first-day comment stuck in the back of my mind.

## MANTRA VS MOTTO

Ok, what's this about?

Mantra vs. motto? Uh, where are you going with this and how does it tie into the content in this book? I would be asking the same questions myself. I asked the same questions not too long ago. I assure you it fits with the content and will be an eye-opener for you (at least I hope).

When we make the first attempts to get into or re-start our fitness journey, we immediately start off with positivity. We search out a lot of positive quotes to help keep us motivated while on our journey. What we think about it is important. Oh, this is so good! If we don't have positive thoughts about our endeavor, we'll more than likely fall off quickly and not stick to it. We find positive quotes, post them around our homes, in our cars, around our workspaces, we memorize them and recite them religiously.

Some days are better than others and we all need the motivation to keep going when faced with rough days or tough times. So, what do we do? We find the quote that best counters our current mindset and say it repeatedly until we either feel motivated enough to start or continue a workout. Or, we'll say the quote repeatedly until we feel frustrated enough to quit a workout or not start one. Again, some days are better than others. What makes the difference in any situation is our perception or thoughts about it. Keeping a positive outlook by focusing on the goals ahead instead of the pain and/or struggle should be the motivation you need to continue. That doesn't always get us through. Trust me, I know. And I commiserate with those who have been there or are there now.

The positive quotes worked for me about a good two to three weeks. I was all fired up to get them and was pumped to recite them. Reciting them when facing a hard day or a day when my body didn't want to cooperate with my head. But it quickly became unimportant. Saying the words didn't change how I felt on the inside about my situation (especially if I was in a rough spot). I had to understand what was going on to get me over the hump(s). So, being the person I am, I had to dissect and take a microscopic look at what I was doing when repeating the motivational quotes. I concluded that these quotes have become mantras for the masses who need motivation.

The word mantra is defined as a statement or slogan repeated frequently especially for motivation or encouragement.

Here are a couple of examples:

'I am not who I'm going to be. I am always becoming.' – Ruby Dee

'The size of your success is measured by the strength of your desire; the size of your dream; and how you handle disappointment along the way." – Robert Kiyosaki

My mantra is 'True transformation is from the inside out. A person does what he thinks.'

Examples:

A motto is a phrase or quote representative of a person or brand's ideals and values. Examples:

'You must do the things you think you cannot do.' – Eleanor Roosevelt

'No one knows what he can do until he tries.' – Publilius Syrus

However, I needed more than a mantra, I needed a motto. One by which I could live by and has become the premise of this book that comes from the Word of

God in Romans 12:2 (KJV) 'And be not conformed to this world: but be ye transformed by the renewing of your mind...'

## BREAKING THE SILENCE
### Self-sabotage/eating disorders?

Today let's break the silence and tell the truth about the things we do to ourselves that cause us to fail and/or fall. Let's remove the masks that society says we must wear. Let's break the chains of bondage that keep us so bound and in fear. Let's say, 'No more. The buck stops here!' I'm so tired of going through the motions and trying to live the lie of a painted smile.

After struggling for so many years with one failure after another, I sat back and took inventory of my actions and what I did to contribute to these failures. I discovered ugly truths about myself and my behavior. If you don't want to stay where you are, you must first accept yourself as you are today. Then, you must own your mistakes and missteps. After that, think back to a time when you failed at something and the circumstances around that failure. Write down everything about it; what you did, thought or hoped for. Then look at the most recent failure, no matter the endeavor, whether you were starting a business or getting back on the horse and getting healthy. Write down everything about this one too.

Do you see a pattern of behavior or thoughts?

What are we being quiet about? Eating disorders and other self-defeating behaviors. Why not just put it out there? I too suffered from an eating disorder. Back in the day, anorexia and bulimia were the only eating disorders talked about. I didn't suffer from either. I loved food and I ate as much as I wanted to, but only at certain times. I was a binge eater. There were no books or clinical studies around this thing. So, I thought it was just me. I knew it was weird, but no one else was talking about it, so I kept quiet.

I noticed a pattern or cycle of eating everything that wasn't nailed down for about two to three weeks and then eating next to nothing for another two to three weeks. It started in my late teens and continued through my early to late thirties. A long time I know, but again there weren't any support groups for this (at least not when I identified it). So, all those years, that was a very personal secret I kept to myself. When I saw the first article about it, not too long ago, I was like, 'It's about time!'

I'm sure that binge-eating isn't quite as devastating as bulimia or anorexia, but it still hurts the body. It causes issues with the function of the pancreas and other systems in the body. It's a contributor to weight gain and the body's resistance to weight loss efforts. When in starvation mode, the body stores fat to keep itself from dying. When in eating mode, the ingested fat is added to the stored fat and what you now have is fat-on-fat. Yo-yo dieting has the same effect. This type of eating and dieting also causes health concerns for the heart.

I had a friend in junior high that suffered from anorexia. She was always thick or heavy, but one of the sweetest people you could ever meet. At the beginning of ninth grade, she came back to school after summer break at least three sizes smaller. We were all shocked. I had heard that she spent time in the hospital over the summer, so I chalked it up as she lost all the weight because she was sick. Little did I know that anorexia was a real sickness and that she suffered with it. She looked almost ghostly; dark circles under her eyes, skin pale and often shiny with sweat. She would be in the bathroom crying uncontrollably. I thought she had cancer or something, so I never mentioned it to her or anyone else. She continued to lose weight and looked even sicker. She was no longer the happy person I had grown to know of the past couple of years. She missed a lot of school initially. I got worried. Again, I thought she had cancer or something. So, I asked her about her condition and offered to help her as much as I could. She broke down and cried long and hard and it broke my heart.

So, I waited for my friend to get through the tears enough to talk and when she told me what she had been dealing with, I cried too. She told me about the doctors she had been seeing and the support group she and her parents attended. I encouraged her to keep doing everything required to get through it. I realized in that moment that how we see ourselves will make us do things to fit in or look like everybody else can hurt us. I told her she was beautiful the way she was before the sickness. But she had a choice to make; either she would continue to let the sickness win and eventually die or she would accept herself and live. She struggled to get better throughout the rest of the school year. Praise report – after the summer break and we entered the new school year, she was back a little bigger than she was the previous year, but not as small and sickly. She was healthy and fit. She was working with a nutritionist and exercising regularly. She looked great and kept up the progress throughout our high school years.

That's two examples of eating disorders, but not all. You can look up studies on them all and read about people who have overcome them.

The other self-defeating behavior I want to address here is self-sabotage.

Huh? What? How can I sabotage myself? Why would I want to? It all goes back to what you think of you. How do you feel about yourself?

What indicates that we have self-sabotaging tendencies?

Have you ever been given the good news of an opportunity and got excited about it at first and then as time went on you became overly anxious about it and never followed through? I have. I used to talk myself out of trying new things to do better because I thought I would look silly and people would laugh. When I dieted and exercised, I eventually find excuses for why I couldn't go to the gym or eat the right foods to reach my goals. I would let others talk me out of doing what I needed to do for myself. I would cheat on my diets. I would buy cakes, cookies and pies (oh my) and eat them while in the car before I got home. I would front about my progress, even when the scale would tell the truth. I would eventually give up and not do anything. Or I would see the small changes and celebrate by rewarding myself with food (the goodies on the do not eat list). I would eat that one extra piece of bread, cake, or whatever as a reward. I would go the gym and not put real effort into a workout. For instance, I would get on the treadmill and walk forty-five mins to an hour four times per week initially. When I made progress, I would slack up and do twenty to thirty mins on the treadmill two times per week. I would go from drinking a gallon of water a day to drinking forty ounces, then down to twenty-five ounces every other day. I would replace the water intake with coffee, tea, and flavored water, knowing full well that the coffee and tea must be replaced with the same fluid ounces of water to keep the body properly hydrated. It's amazing how we fool ourselves into thinking that we're pulling the wool over someone's eyes when we're stunting our own growth and possibilities.

I never thought that dieting could be enjoyable. I was always under the impression it had to be a hard thing and a person had to struggle through it. Had I known all the good, tasty foods I could eat and still be dieting, I would have won this battle a loooong time ago.

But knowing what I know now makes the difference. Food need not be bland and blah to be good for you. Some foods that are bland and blah aren't good for you. So, don't be like me and think that diet food must be the worst food ever.

Embrace the fact that a healthy diet has good taste and is good for you. There are many recipes you can use to make healthy eating a habit and not a chore. If you think of it as a chore, you won't enjoy it and you definitely won't stick to it.

If you change your mind about the food choices you have as a dieter, you'll be able to stick to your program and reach your goals. To get better acquainted with eating healthy foods, try cooking a simple recipe, go to a class and sample what's offered or have friends over and you all make a dish and sample them together. It can be great fun. I'm just throwing out some suggestions to help you get out of thinking the worst about healthy eating. It's not dieting done for a short period. Healthy eating is a lifestyle that needs to be adopted by everyone whether you must lose weight or not.

## YOUR TRUTH

When you meet new people, what do you tell them about yourself? What about when you go to the gym or a group exercise class? Does the content of your conversation change? Most people in a gym setting focus their conversations on why they're there. You may hear things like, 'I want to get the extra weight off for an upcoming event'; 'I'm way too big and want to lose [x] amount of weight'; 'I can't fit into my big clothes, so I want to go down a couple of dress/pants sizes' or 'I wouldn't be so big if they'd stop making donuts, etc.'. This list could go on because everyone has their own reasons for wanting to exercise. But can you see those reasons stated in a positive manner? Meaning, do the reasons listed appear that the person speaking loves himself/herself? Or does the speaker sound like they have a bad body image? It's not always what people say that makes the difference. It's what their bodies are saying. Are you aware of the non-verbal messages you give when you talk about yourself? What does your body language say about you?

What we say about ourselves is what we believe ourselves to be or is our reality of ourselves. Our insecurities due to bad body image can hinder our journey to better health and fitness if we allow them to. Some people do things to avoid conversations about weight. They may become visibly upset when conversations turn to the subject of weight. Some say nothing or change the subject altogether. Some people, like me, will make a joke about their size or the foods they eat, etc. This tactic of avoidance or redirection and others like that are forms of defense. Some people are very sensitive about their weight because of the struggles they may have had or have with their weight. Either way, weight is a topic that never seems to get old. So, instead of becoming defensive, shy away from, change the subject or even crack a joke; why not address the elephant in the room (no not you, the subject).

There are people who can talk freely about their journey and the issues they've encountered along the way while others can't. I've heard that the best way to confront an issue is to talk about it, then counter its effect on your life. Easier said than done, but yet and still very POSSIBLE! But before you can overcome any obstacle, you must know its origin. How did your bad body image begin? Did it start while you were in school, at an event, while in a relationship, from a mean or negative comment, etc.? Where did your truth begin for you?

While I'm not an expert or professional psychologist, after countless conversations with others in the struggle, from many different articles read, and various trainings for health and fitness professionals, I've found there are some basic factors that we all have in common. Not saying that every individual situation isn't uniquely different from others, but there are a few common denominators. Let's look at some of them now.

1. Historical relationship with food: from childhood and family perspective
   a. How was food perceived in your childhood?
   b. Was food used for comfort, reward or was strict dieting a part of your family's perspective of food?
   c. Did you have more than enough food in the home or did you have little?
2. Relationships: family, friends, and romantic interests

   a. Were you teased as a child by siblings or other family members? It doesn't matter if you were big/heavy as a child but being teased (constantly) just because is a contributing factor to your truth.

   b. Were your friends always going on diets or talking about exercise a lot?

   c. Did/ do your romantic interests concern themselves about your size or hint around about your size/weight?

3. Medical history: hereditary conditions, past health conditions,

   a. Are you predisposed to diseases based on your family history, diseases such as hypertension, diabetes, heart disease, cancer?

   b. Have you been or are you currently taking medication that affects your weight?

   c. Was healthy living a priority in the home?

4. Media: marketing ads, movies, tv shows, celebrities

   a. Do you feel compelled to try the latest and greatest celebrity endorsed product promoted?

- b. Do you feel compelled to become as close in size to your most favored celebrity?
- c. Do you feel guilty or pressured to change your appearance after watching ads on tv or seeing other media ads of people working out, eating healthy, wearing swimsuits?

These are some things that are contributing factors to developing our truths. I'm sure that you could probably think of more, but let's look closely at what we have.

1. Historical relationship with food: from childhood and family perspective
   - a. The importance placed on food in our childhood determines how we see it now. Either you eat to live or live to eat.
   - b. Using food to comfort children has been done throughout the ages. I know you see it on tv and in movies when the woman is depressed or upset, she goes to the freezer and gets a pint or half gallon container of ice cream and a big spoon. They show men do the same but only as a spoof on women. Sad? Yes. Funny? No. Because many

people don't know how to find comfort outside of self-destructing avenues. Ice cream binging self-destructive? Girl, you've gone off the deep end on this one.

**Example:** a diabetic person gets depressed and chooses the oh so comforting bucket of ice cream; blood sugar shoots through the roof. This is unhealthy and unsafe for any diabetic especially if done more than once, whether using insulin to regulate or pills. The risk of taking more medication than prescribed is caused by this behavior.

Let's say the person has no medical issues and goes through the same scenario. Ok, they've eaten half of the bucket (no matter the size) of ice cream. Say this happens more than once a month or they're going through something and this ice cream eating goes on for a couple of days or weeks even. What happens to this person's weight and size? Goes up, right? Well, they had no issue, but now they must deal with additional weight and buy different sized clothes to wear. So, tell me again, what were the benefits of the ice cream binge?  Outside of the temporary lift, none.  This scenario could spiral in too many ways.  But I think you get the picture, at least I hope you do.

Was food used to celebrate occasions outside of regular holidays?  Whenever we wanted to do something special for the team at work, we'd go out to eat or prepare food and bring it in, set it up and eat throughout the day.  We center activities around food to celebrate birthdays, promotions, friendly get-togethers, family time, graduations, etc.

Was there a certain food type that wasn't allowed in the home (sweets, candy, salt, etc.) due to diet restrictions?  So, a person may make food choices with the attitude that they're making up for lost time based on what they couldn't have as a child.

c.  Did you grow up in a household where the financial struggles meant there wasn't an abundance of food in the house except maybe during holidays (if that)?  Again, some people make food choices with the attitude of making up for lost time for the things they didn't have when growing up.

Did you grow up in a household where there was so much food it was actually wasted? If so, a person may overbuy food and waste it regularly. They may even cook more than they need and it goes to waste.

2. Relationship: family, friends and romantic interest
   a. Did family members like to tease a lot? We all teased each other in a good-natured way in my family. We still do. Everyone knew that once the family got together, there would be a lot of laughter. No one particular person was targeted, everyone was a target. We would warn any guests that would come of potentially becoming a victim of the family fun. We would tease each other about things from a facial expression to the color of your clothes. We even talked about your kids, especially if there was a newborn. That child could be the most beautiful baby ever, but we

would still tease about the size of their head, feet, nose, ears, etc. And if that didn't get a good enough laugh, we would swear the baby didn't look like the father and accuse the mother of hooking up with the mailman. I teased other family members about their weight and size because I was always smaller than everyone else. Boy, did that came back and bite me in the behind! I had gained weight after having children and I was the same size as everybody that I had teased. It didn't feel good, but I couldn't complain because of how much I teased others. It made me take a long hard look at myself and what I thought needed to change. I was looking from the outside and all I could see were the physical changes to be made. If I had this reaction, I could only imagine what others felt like when I teased them. It didn't feel good, even for a few laughs. So, I experienced first-hand the effects of body shaming; both as giver and recipient.

b. Were your friends or the people you hung around with always talking about weight and issues around it? I knew girls in school absolutely obsessed with weight. These were the cheerleaders in junior high and high school. You couldn't converse with one without the conversation getting centered on weight. They would talk about the weight they planned to lose before x, y, z game, event or competition. Some girls were super slim and yet there were a few who weren't so slim. These gave their all and had all the confidence in the world. Nothing seemed to bother them unless uncaring individuals would bring up weight in conversations. There was this one girl who wasn't slim or small and yet she was a superstar in my book. She had tried to fit in and dieted when the rest of the girls suggested it. She didn't lose much but was only more frustrated with every failed attempt. So, what did she do? Did she quit? No, she didn't quit. She came back with the attitude she was the size she was and happy to be who she was and not try to fit the mold they were trying to put her in. She claimed her independence from the herd and moved on to shine so brightly that she was the team captain the following year.

c. Have you ever been in a relationship where the other person would hint at weight issues and dieting? Some people think that it's okay to openly say that you don't fit their idea of healthy by the way you look and expect you to change for them. Yeah, I know what you're thinking. I had such a person in my life once. I even tried to fit the image they expected of me (didn't make it). I had an ex that told me (at size sixteen) that I had to be at least a size ten before he would marry me. Uh, yeah. He said that. What did I do you ask? I worked out, I dieted and took every kind of something that promised to melt the fat off. I'm not proud of that, but it's the truth. We got married (I was a size twelve) understanding that I would continue to work towards that size ten (he really wanted a size eight but he would compromise). That relationship didn't last long, once I woke up out of my low self-esteem induced coma. A story for another day.

Anyway, you can see how people will try to change how you look based on their own ideals. There are people who may not be as blunt as the person described above, but they still do and say things that hint at what they want you to do to fit their bill.

3. Medical history: hereditary conditions, past health conditions
    a. Are there any health conditions or diseases that run in your family? Diabetes, hypertension (high blood pressure), cancer, high cholesterol or heart disease are things that can be hereditary diseases that can cause unwanted weight gain or weight loss. Being unhealthy isn't always for the overweight person. Thin or slim people can be unhealthy. But if you have these or any disease, the medicines

prescribed to control them can cause weight gain of which you have no control over. However, you still have control over your health. Huh? As you stay in compliance with prescribed meds, proper diet, and adequate exercise, you can be at your healthiest even with the disease. Some people control hypertension and diabetes just by diet and exercise and eventually moving to lesser medication to no medication. That depends on an individual working closely with his/her physician and nutritionist.

b. If you've had a previous condition that required you to take certain medications that caused weight gain, there's nothing that you can do about that, except be at your healthiest even after the condition has gone. I'm talking about conditions like cancer (now in remission), transplants (anti-rejection medications cause tremendous weight gain) and other issues like allergy flare-ups which may require a regimen of steroids to control that cause weight gain.

c. Were your parents or the people in the home you grew up in health conscious? Were you served standard portions and encouraged to not eat unhealthy snacks? Were snacks like chips, chocolate, soda, etc. not allowed in the house? Some families with members with illnesses or diseases base food shopping and meals around the particular diet of the one affected by the illness or disease. If you grew up in a household like this, you are more likely to become lax in your approach to what foods you eat. Not all people rebel in such a subtle fashion, there are many people who carry on the what they learned about food and nutrition from home. There's nothing wrong with that. I just want you to see how this could affect the development of your truth.

4. Media: marketing ads, movies, tv shows, celebrities

a. Do you have a favorite celebrity you may follow on social media or any other information system? Or have you seen the infomercials with celebrities singing the praises of products on late night tv? What about the talk show hosts that hawk products on their shows? Once, I can remember when Dr. Oz rarely suggested products on his show. It seemed as if he either tested the products personally or had them tested before he would make any suggestions. He became a trusted friend of the television audience and people took his word as truth. Look at how many products are marketed on his show and the shows of others who have gained the trust of the public. I'm not saying that the products aren't tested. I'm saying look at how the public buys these products based on the suggestions of these celebrities. It's the influence of a person you may trust that contributes to your truth.
b. Do you have someone you admire and desire to become more like them? You

may never be like them but you could try to look like them. There are people all over the world who have surgeries to look like their idols. Look at the woman who had herself turned into a living Barbie. What about the lady who had herself changed into a human version of a cat? The changes on the outside don't change who these people are on the inside. I'm not saying that all people go to these great lengths to become like someone they admire. Some people may change the way they dress, what they eat, where they shop, etc. to be more like their idol. This too can affect the development of your truth.

c. Have you ever gotten lax with your exercise program and instead of going to the gym you just laid around and watched tv? Only while watching tv, an ad for a new gym or exercise program comes on and you're like, 'I really should have gone to the gym today. I'll definitely do it tomorrow.' Has that ever happened to you? It's happened to me too often to count.  Or how about when you're out driving and you go past the park you normally go to work out, and there are many people there working out and you're just riding by?  Did you feel guilty about that?  Did it even move you?  Did you say to yourself, 'Definitely tomorrow'?  These things and your reaction to them also contribute to developing your truth.

When you look at the information in this section, you can see that, yes, some things are common bonds when it comes to how our self-images are developed.  What we do with the knowledge gained here will determine how successful we become in our pursuits of anything worth chasing in our lives.  It's not limited to healthy living and being fit.

## GOD'S TRUTH OF YOU

As discussed in the previous section, your truth is based on the things that helped develop your self-image. While these things very well may be the deciding factors in who you've become, they may not be true. You see how we see ourselves may be from a skewed viewpoint or perspective as opposed to how God sees us.

I don't want to sound preachy or anything but knowing that having a distorted self-image is the primary factor in any failures you've experienced in life. Remember, true transformation begins within -- your mind! People do or approach things in life by what they think. Your mind must be changed. If you don't believe that you're unique and special in your own way, then you must be reminded that when a perfect God created you, He created you perfectly.

You must see yourself as the beautiful creation God made you to be. I encourage you to dig into His Word to find His truth of you because His truth is the only truth that matters. So, as we read through some of the Biblical scriptures read with an open mind and a willingness to accept and apply those scriptures to yourself. How to do that is to read them, speak them, write them, cry them if you must but don't just skim over them and forget them. These are your weapons against your worst critic – you.

When you talk yourself out of doing the right things, speak God's truth about you. When you feel like giving u on the next workout and giving into the temptation of just laying around – read what God has to say about His great love for you.

When you want to just quit everything, think about how God has never given up on you.

When you believe that you're in this by yourself and no one understands, remember that God has never left you and He is always there watching over you.

When you feel weak and want those extra-large fries from your favorite hamburger joint, don't forget that God gives you strength.

The scriptures are a great source of strength for me, whether I read, speak, think or sing them. I find myself empowered by them when I go to them first when I feel weak, tired or tempted. You may not have the same experiences I do, I'm just encouraging you as a believer to try. Nothing beats a try but a failure. All failures aren't meant to keep you down, some strengthen your resolve to complete, finish or overcome something. I challenge you right here, right now to use the power of God's words about you to encourage yourself daily.

If you never walk away with anything from this book or section, walk away with knowing that God loves you with an everlasting love. Know that God loves you so much He gave His only Son to die for you so you can have a personal relationship with Him. Now that's love! Which of your friends or family members would give up an only child just to have a relationship with you? Something to think about. Anyway, I digress. Back to the task at hand.

So, just thinking about those two statements about God's love for you should be enough to intrigue you to know more.

Here are a few scriptures I have found useful in my transformation process:

**Jeremiah 31:3 (ESV)**

…..I have loved you with an everlasting love; therefore I have continued my faithfulness to you.

**John 3:16 (ESV)**

For God so loved the world that he gave his only Son that whoever believes in him should not perish but have eternal life.

**Romans 5:8 (ESV)**

God shows his love for us in that while we were still sinners, Christ died for us.

**1 John 3:1 (ESV)**

See what kind of love the Father has given to us, that we should we called children of God; and so we are.

**Isaiah 41:10 (ESV)**

Fear not, for I am with you; be not dismayed, for I am your God; I will strengthen you, I will help you, I will uphold you with my righteous right hand.

**Psalm 139:14 (ESV)**

I praise you, for I am fearfully and wonderfully made. Wonderful are your works; my soul knows it very well.

**Lamentations 3:22-23 (ESV)**

The steadfast love of the LORD never ceases; his mercies never come to an end; they are new every morning...

**Isaiah 49:16 (ESV)**

Behold, I have engraved you in the palms of my hands; your walls are continually before me.

**Psalm 63:3 (ESV)**

Because your steadfast love is better than life, my lips will praise you.

**Psalm 147:3 (ESV)**

He heals the brokenhearted and binds up their wounds.

**1 John 4:9 (ESV)**

In this the love of God was made manifest among us, that God sent his only Son into the world, so that we might live through him.

**Isaiah 43:4 (ESV)**

Because you are precious in my eyes, and honored and I love you...

**1 John 3:16 (ESV)**

By this we know love, that he laid down his life for us...

**1 John 4:16 (NIV)**

And so we know and rely on the love God has for us.

## RENEWING THE MIND

Now that we have read about God's love for us. There's something else in His Word that is the driving force or factor of this book. Let's look at it and push forward. I promise not to go too deep into it, but the message is abundantly clear. Here, read it for yourself:

**Romans 12:2 (NLT)**

Don't copy the behavior and customs of this world, but let God transform you into a new person by changing the way you think

When our truth doesn't meet God's truth of us, we need to have a mind change or change of mind.

I mentioned in the last section that when we read, write, pray or speak the scriptures regularly, our thoughts of ourselves change. We see ourselves as God sees us – loved.

So, if God loves us so much to repeat it several times in His Word, how can we then say that there's something we don't like about ourselves?

According to the scripture, true transformation comes from changing the way we think. I'm not telling you to memorize the entire Bible or even the scriptures from the previous section. All I'm suggesting is that as you read down the list, find 1, 2, 3 or 5 and use them just as you have used daily affirmations and positivity quotes.

Once you speak the scriptures, in the places where it states 'you', say 'me' and 'I'. For example:

Romans 2:12 (NLT)

Don't copy the behavior and customs of this world, but let God transform 'me' into a new person by changing the way 'I' think.

You can even turn it into an affirmation:

'I won't copy the behavior and customs of this world, but I will let God transform me into a new person by changing the way I think.'

Whichever works for you, try it. Please keep track of your progress in a journal. You'll be amazed at how knowing you are 'loved' impacts your life! True transformation is inevitable when you apply God's Word to your life.

**YOUR 'BILL OF RIGHTS'**

As you begin to be renewed in the inner man, know that you have rights that no one can take from you.

**YOU HAVE THE RIGHT TO...**
BE HAPPY
BE AT PEACE
LET GO OF NEGATIVE PEOPLE
EMBRACE LOVE
BE YOUR SELF
LOVE LIFE
LIVE YOUR FAITH
BE FREE
CELEBRATE THE LITTLE THINGS
FORGIVE YOURSELF
DO WHAT YOU LOVE
FOLLOW YOUR DREAMS
PRACTICE YOUR PASSION
MAKE MISTAKES
LEARN AND GROW FROM YOUR MISTAKES
BE SUCCESSFUL
CHANGE BAD HABITS
BE GREAT EVERY DAY
LOVE WHO YOU ARE NOW

LOVE WHO YOU ARE BECOMING
ENCOURAGE AND EMPOWER OTHERS
SHARE YOUR JOY

**BE TRANS4MED 4LIFE**

## GETTING OVER YOURSELF

If you've never used daily affirmations or positivity quotes, getting started can be a little intimidating. You will feel silly (I know I did) at first. You get comfortable after a while especially when you believe what you're saying aren't just words to be repeated, but the words describe who you are becoming.

Now that you've begun to daily affirm God's truth, you're on your way to true transformation. Yes? Yes and no.

The daily affirmations created from the scriptures are vitally important to the changed mind you need to be transformed. But somewhere along the way, there's a trap set for you and it's called complacency.

*According to Merriam Webster's Dictionary 'complacency' means self-satisfaction especially when accompanied by unawareness of actual dangers or deficiencies.*

Sometimes, you will want to reward yourself with a break from your routine. This isn't a problem, I even recommend decreasing the frequency and/or intensity of workouts when you feel the need. The problem is when you take a break, you stop doing everything. You may think to yourself, 'I've made this much progress towards my goals and I deserve some time off.' That's all fine and good, just remember not to extend the break to where you actually must start over. I did that and it was not the best idea that I've ever had (it wasn't the worst either). But it had a major impact on me, both physically and mentally.

I got to where I wanted and thought I desperately needed a break. So, I took one. At first, I felt guilty, like I had abandoned my dreams and let my family down. Because once you stop everything, you go back to old (bad) eating habits and gradually decreasing from daily exercising to none …well you can guess there was a giant leap backward. Sad but true, but I've been there and done that! Do I say that with pride? Heck no! Am I ashamed of it? I was at first, but again it's my journey. I can only share what I've learned from the good and the bad choices I've made. Did I always eat bad food during my break? No. I felt bad enough to at least eat the better foods.

Why am I sharing this? I'm sharing this so you have a real example of what this journey to true transformation is like. It's not automatic nor is it instantaneous. It takes focus, determination, and the support of family and friends.

So, when you get to where you want to take a break, re-read this section.

In actuality, it's a lot harder to start over once you've taken time off than it is to just suck it up and continue to push through.

Why is it harder? It's harder because you remember the muscle aches and soreness you experienced when you started the first time. You must rearrange your schedule to include gym time or time at home to exercise. You may think of other reasons to put that restart on the back burner, but again, I'm sharing my journey; the good and the bad.

Once I revisited my *why* I had to apologize to myself for allowing distractions to help me lose focus. How does this happen? When you take your focus off of your *why* and focus on the mechanics of the process (exercise, eat right), you do the lone-wolf method and don't use your support system, or you take on too many projects and just never get to squeeze in the workout you promised yourself.

What's the remedy when this happens? Nip it in the bud! When you *feel* overwhelmed with your routine or it becomes stale, go back to your *why*, call a support person, repeat the affirmations and look for other workouts or add different exercises to your routine to keep it fresh. Most of the time, your trainer can help keep your workouts fresh and exciting.

To avoid this pitfall or misdirection while on your journey, it's best to keep your *why* posted where you can see it regularly, especially while you're working out. Keeping your why visible will help motivate you to keep going when you get tired or weary. Keep it posted where you prep and eat your meals (even if those are different areas) so you don't lose focus and eat the wrong things.

Keep your affirmations posted. Put them on your mirrors, on the fridge, at your desk or workstation, in the car, you can even record them and set a reminder to listen to them daily. Keep a food journal. Drink the water – straight; no chaser. Infused water is good also, but you must drink it for it to benefit your body. Contact your support system. Get a buddy to workout with or an accountability partner. This works well for those of us who are competitive. It makes it fun to challenge one another all the while pushing you closer to your goals.

These things will work if utilized, but it all comes down to what you think about it.

I've gotten over myself and incorporated trips to the gym weekly and adding at-home workouts. I'm picking up where I've left off and pushing forward.

**YOUR TESTIMONY**

As you share your story with others, it encourages you to continue on your journey. When you feel like quitting or giving up, you see how what you share inspires others to either start on their own journey, continue what they've started or even get back on track.

It all comes down to how you share your experience.

Everyone isn't a public speaker, but I'm not telling you to book a hall or stadium and get on stage with a mic and tell your story. I'm talking about in conversations with people you talk to daily. You can best believe that people are watching you. Whether they're watching to see if you fall or if they notice anything. Remember, you didn't begin your journey of transformation for people to see the image of you. You want them to see who you're becoming. The differences will show, some more quickly than others, but transformation will become manifest in you. It's all for the best.

Your testimony not only helps others, but it helps you. When you talk about how you're not the same person as you once were, and how you overcame the obstacles in your path, you realize just how much every part of the journey was really worth the trip.

Now, no one is perfect and we all must still fight every day to maintain, but as you see the changes in yourself, you'll want to share with people. Especially with those you love, who may have issues of their own that they either can't address or won't address. Don't beat people over the head with your accomplishments. Stay humble and share if anyone asks about any changes they see in you. So, let conversations flow naturally into the direction of changes you've made and what it is that you've done to achieve your health/fitness goals. If given the opportunity to share your story with a group of people, then do so. And take the opportunity to be honest about the ups/downs and in/outs of your transformation process. Believe me, someone will benefit from your honesty and zeal.

This portion and every other part of this book were written for you. So, that when the days/nights come when you just can't find the motivation to continue, you'll be encouraged to step out of your comfort zone and share your experience about your journey and what you've accomplished watch how it makes you feel.  Amazing!

I want much feedback regarding this part of your journey when you get to it.  I look forward to many wonderful stories of lives being changed just because you shared your testimony.

## YOUR COMMUNITY – WE'RE IN THIS TOGETHER

Never think that you're the only person going through what you're going through, whether you're at the beginning of your journey or have been on your journey for a while, there's still someone who has been where you are.

We've all started by seeing and feeling the need for change in our lives if we are going to love ourselves completely. We acknowledged the need, we planned to change and researched everything we could find about it. We all want better for ourselves and our loved ones. We've all planned to start, whether we did is another story altogether. Anyway, we thought change was what we needed. Yes and no. We needed to change what we said and did to reach goals we set without knowledge of the need for transformation.

I knew that I needed to change what I did to get back into shape for my health, so I researched some of the local gyms. Then there were FB friends all posting about a particular gym and how much they loved it and the pics they posted showed amazing results or transformations as they were called. So, what did I do, but join? I had begun to adjust my food choices, etc. I was getting back on track and again working on my program and wanted to be in a position to endure a workout session without being embarrassed. I thought this six-week program would be the kick start I needed. I was right! The workouts were rough. They made me challenge myself and I had pain in places I had forgotten existed. You'd think that the more you work out, the better you'd feel. Well, each day was a different set of exercises for different parts of the body. So, every day had its own set of pain. I lost little weight during the six weeks, but I lost some inches. I fit into clothes I hadn't worn in four years. They fit so much better. So, I didn't get discouraged. I was more excited than anything. When the double chin became one chin, it took me by surprise. I couldn't stop talking about how much energy I had and all the wonderful things that go along with exercising regularly. I didn't realize how much I missed it until then.

Anyway, when you've decided to get into shape you make the time to do it. You make the sacrifices it takes to get there.

So, you're not alone from beginning to end. The only difference between you and others who have made the same decision is the why.

What motivates you? What are you trying to accomplish? Who are you trying to become?

Our initial motivation may dwindle as we sweat in grueling workouts. When your feet say, "Get off me!" And your knees say, "We quit!"

What is it that keeps you going? So, when these things happen and your body begins to question your sanity, don't feel bad. We've all been there.

## CONCLUSION

Keeping in the spirit of being transparent and authentic, I must tell you that during the time it has taken to go through the writing process for this work, I had stopped working out and sometimes ate the wrong things. I didn't beat myself up about it. I can say that without condemnation or guilt because my mind hadn't changed about how I feel about me.

Distractions come in many disguises, and once I recognized that I had given fully into the distractions of life I was shocked. The main distraction came in exhaustion. I had little energy to do anything but go to work, church, and home. I would get home from work and basically pass out from exhaustion.

Yes, I got offset, but that didn't keep me from finishing what I started.

Many times, I almost gave up writing this, but I was determined to finish. I realize this pursuit of better health and fitness is a lifelong journey. I say lifelong because once you reach your goals, you must maintain no matter what comes your way.

If you think that I have failed during this phase of my journey, then you've missed the point and purpose of this book.

This isn't a book about exercise and dieting. This is a book about true transformation from the inside out. The transformation isn't dependent upon whether you meet a set of fitness or dieting goals. This transformation is contingent upon your mind changing about how you feel about you! Do you love yourself more today because of what you read in this book? Or do you feel the same? Do you understand more about why you think the way you do? Do you see yourself through a different set of eyes?

The insights in this work are ones that can be used in every area of life. Every goal you set for personal and/or professional growth and development can be achieved using them.

I love myself just as I am and there's room for improvement for my health's sake, but the fact that I don't beat myself up about falling off for a bit is proof of my own trans4mation.

It is my prayer you have been inspired and empowered to embark on your own journey to true trans4mation while using the insights provided in this book While on your journey, do not fear because you have weapons in your arsenal to fight every obstacle, distraction, and argument that will come your way.

Just know that your success is determined by your mindset. So, let your mind be changed by God's truth of who you are. Be patient with yourself and note your progress. You are well on your way to true transformation.

www.ingramcontent.com/pod-product-compliance
Lightning Source LLC
Chambersburg PA
CBHW051704090426
42736CB00013B/2528